CAMBRIDGE SKILLS FOR FLUENCY
Series Editor: Adrian Doff

Listening 2
TEACHER'S BOOK

Adrian Doff

Published by the Press Syndicate of the University of Cambridge
The Pitt Building, Trumpington Street, Cambridge CB2 1RP
40 West 20th Street, New York, NY 10011–4211, USA
10 Stamford Road, Oakleigh, Melbourne 3166, Australia

© Cambridge University Press 1994

First published 1994

Printed in Great Britain
at the University Press, Cambridge

ISBN 0 521 47871 5 Teacher's Book
ISBN 0 521 36748 4 Student's Book
ISBN 0 521 36545 7 Set of 2 cassettes

Copyright
The law allows a reader to make a single copy of part of a book for purposes of private study. It does not allow the copying of entire books or the making of multiple copies of extracts. Written permission for any such copying must always be obtained from the publisher in advance.

Contents

Introduction 4
1 Music in the mind 6
2 Strangers in the street 7
3 Embarrassing moments 8
4 Conversations in public 9
5 Views 11
6 On the line 12
7 Intruders 14
8 Childhood 15
9 Bought and sold 16
10 Behind the picture 18
11 Believe it or not 19
12 Bread and mushrooms 21
13 Learning to draw 22
14 Male and female 23
15 Bees 25
16 Emergency 26
17 Punishing children 27
18 Planet Earth 29
19 Sporting moments 30
20 War zones 32

Introduction

At the end of *Listening 2* Student's Book there is a general description of the aims and features of the book. The teaching notes contained in this book give more detailed information about the units and how to use them. They include:
- a brief description of the aim of each activity;
- a list of key vocabulary and new words that appear in the recordings;
- step-by-step instructions for doing the activities;
- answers to the exercises.

Structure of the book

THE UNITS
Listening 2 has 20 units. They are completely self-contained, so units can be used separately from each other.

The units are divided into two parts, A and B. Each part has enough material for about 30–45 minutes of listening and other class activities. In most units, the two parts are separate, but they are linked by topic; this means that they can be used on their own or the two parts can be used together. In a few units (13, 14, 15, 17) the two parts are more closely connected, and develop a single theme.

LEVEL
The units follow a rough order of difficulty. The early units are intended to be fairly easy, with a lot of help given to the student; it should be possible to use them with students at low-intermediate level or below. As you work through the book, the units gradually become more difficult, and the later units go slightly beyond intermediate level.

Using the book

PRE-LISTENING ACTIVITIES
The listening activities nearly always begin with a *pre-listening stage*. This stage is important and is worth spending time on for several reasons:
- it gives students a chance to start thinking about the topic and to become familiar with it before they start listening to the tape;
- it is a way of bringing the topic to life and involving students in it, so that they will be more motivated to listen;
- it helps them to predict what they are going to hear, and this makes listening to the tape easier;
- it is a chance to focus on key vocabulary that students will need to understand;
- it is a chance for students to speak and use English, instead of just listening passively to it.

The teaching notes give detailed suggestions for using the pre-listening stage in each unit.

PLAYING THE TAPE
Most of the recordings are either short, or are divided into short sections. This means that you can easily play them more than once, and if necessary several times. How often you need to play the tape, of course, depends on the level of your class. Detailed suggestions are given in the unit-by-unit notes, but here is a basic procedure:
1 Play the tape once, either right through or pausing after sections. Students answer questions.
2 *Optional stage:* If students can't answer all the questions, play the tape a second, and possibly a third time.
3 Go through the answers together. As you do this, play the tape again. Pause at points where the answers occur, and focus on what the speaker said.
4 *Optional stage:* If students still haven't understood everything, play the tape once again. This time let students follow the tapescript as they listen.

LISTENING FOR THE GENERAL IDEA AND LISTENING FOR DETAILS
Often the listening is divided into two stages:
- *Listening for the general idea.* Students listen and answer one or two general questions. At this stage students do not need to understand everything, and shouldn't try to.
- *Listening for details.* Students listen again, and answer more detailed questions, which focus on particular points in the recording. By the end of this stage, students should understand most of what they hear; if they don't, give more help with vocabulary or let them look at the tapescript.

DEALING WITH VOCABULARY
In some listening activities, there is an area of key vocabulary which is important for understanding the tape (e.g. types of fast food in Unit 2B; telephone expressions in Unit 6B; names of ingredients in Unit 12A). Often these words are given on the page in the exercise itself, so that

Introduction

they can be dealt with before students hear the tape. In the vocabulary box in the teaching notes, these words are listed under the heading *Key vocabulary*.

There are also other words and phrases which students may not know, and which may cause difficulties when listening to the tape. They are listed in the teaching notes under the heading *New words and phrases*. The teaching notes include ideas for when and how to present these items.

There are several ways of dealing with unknown words:
- *Present them beforehand*, during the pre-listening stage. This is a good time to present key words and expressions which are essential to understanding the tape.
- *Present them while going through answers*. The questions and tasks focus on key points on the tape. So when you go through the answers you can easily check whether students understand important words and phrases.
- *Focus on them afterwards*. When students have understood the main ideas on the tape, you can play it again, focusing on particular words and phrases that are hard to understand. Often there is a special exercise in the unit which does this.

GRAMMATICAL STRUCTURES

The activities in this book are intended to develop listening skills, as part of students' general fluency in English – they are *not* intended as a means of practising grammatical structures. In general, grammatical structures are not likely to cause students serious problems in understanding the tape, and it is worth paying more attention to vocabulary than to structures.

EXTENSION ACTIVITIES

These are optional, and provide an opportunity for students to say things themselves which are similar to what they have heard on the tape. Sometimes they are games or short role-plays, sometimes students talk about their own experiences or find out information from each other.

The teaching notes suggest ways of using these activities, and include ideas for using them with large classes.

We hope these teaching notes will help you and your students to get the most out of using the activities in *Listening 2*.

Adrian Doff

1 Music in the mind

A Mental images

Students listen to some Japanese koto music, and hear five people saying what comes to their mind as they listen to it.

> **Key vocabulary**
>
> See words listed in Stage 2 below.
>
> *Other new words*
>
> steamy   landscape
> Arabian   hopeless
> fan   cosy
> outside   arrangements
> chill

STAGE 1: LISTENING TO THE MUSIC
- Tell the class you will play them some music, but do not say what it is. Ask them to let a picture come into their minds as they listen, and to write down three words that describe the picture. If you like, give an example (e.g. *rain, umbrella, wet*).
- Play the music. Students listen and write down their words.

STAGE 2: LISTENING
- Play the tape, pausing after each section. Students write down three key words from each description. (If necessary, do the first one together, to show students what to do.)
- Pairwork. Students compare their words.
- Discuss the answers together. Build up a list of words on the board, and discuss what country each speaker has in mind.
  Possible answers:
  1 moonlight, elephants, hot (India)
  2 tent, cool, banquet (Saudi Arabia)
  3 travelling, horse, mountains (USA?)
  4 empty, plain, alone (Siberia?)
  5 garden, waterfalls, flowers (Japan?)

STAGES 3 & 4: DISCUSSION
- Pairwork. Students show their words to each other, and describe the picture they saw.
- As a round-up, ask a few students to tell you what their words were.
- Finally, discuss where the music really came from. Explain that koto music is traditional Japanese music, played solo on a stringed instrument. If possible, bring in some pictures of koto players.

B Musical memories

Two people talk about a favourite piece of music and say what associations it has for them. One speaker is British, the other is American.

> *New words and phrases*
>
> make an impact   spring
> as opposed to   breaking
> balmy   shorts
> gallery   festivals
> audience   a good attitude
> bowler hats

STAGE 1: LISTENING
- Look at the pictures and establish what they show. (The Albert Hall is a concert hall, Georgia is in the southern USA.)
- Play the tape and establish the connection between the music and the pictures.
  Answers:
  1 The speaker went to the Albert Hall; it was the first live classical concert he went to.
  2 The music reminds the speaker of spring in Athens, Georgia (his home town).

STAGE 2: LISTENING
- Working alone or in pairs, students guess which items they will hear in each description, and complete the table. Find out if everybody made the same guesses.
- Play the tape. Then go through the table and establish what the real answers were.
  Answers:
  Albert Hall: wandering around, holding hands, paper aeroplanes, newspapers over faces, music drifting upwards
  Athens, Georgia: swimming, blue sky, throwing footballs
  Note: The first speaker is describing a 'promenade concert', a special kind of concert where people can buy cheap tickets but have no seat.

STAGE 3: DISCUSSION
- Choose a type of concert that most students are familiar with (it could be classical, pop, folk music, etc.). Ask students to remember a time they went to a concert of this type (or to imagine what it would be like). Ask how it was different from the Albert Hall concert. Build up a list of descriptive phrases on the board (e.g.

loud music, people clapping their hands, people whistling).
- Ask students to imagine their home town on 1st May. Again, build up a list of descriptive phrases on the board.

STAGE 4: OPTIONAL EXTENSION
- To help with this activity, give students a few minutes' preparation time, in which they think about a favourite piece of music and make brief notes (in English or their own language). Alternatively, ask students to bring a cassette into the next lesson and talk for a few minutes about it.

2 Strangers in the street

A Excuse me…
Four short conversations between strangers, each beginning with an offer or request. This activity gives practice in listening to conversational English and predicting replies.

> **Key expressions: offers and requests**
>
> Would you like to…?
> (Excuse me), can you…?
> I wonder if you could…?
>
> *New words*
>
> | | |
> |---|---|
> | bus fare | organisation |
> | spare | starving |
> | market research | identification |

STAGE 1: PRE-LISTENING FOCUS
- Ask what the people in the pictures are doing (selling a watch, collecting money). Ask students to suggest what they might say, and try to get a range of ideas (e.g. 'Look, sir, a lovely watch', 'Do you need a watch?' '£10 for a beautiful watch').

STAGES 2 & 3: LISTENING
- Play the tape. Students listen and write suitable replies.
- Find out what replies students wrote down.
- Play the tape to establish what the real replies were.

• STAGE 4: LISTENING & DISCUSSION
- Play the complete conversations, pausing after each one. Ask a few questions each time to check that students have understood, e.g.:

  1 How much is the watch? (£9.99, then £8)
    Where does it come from? (Switzerland, so the man says)

  Then discuss the questions on the page.
  Note: These are discussion questions, with no right or wrong answers. Get a range of opinions, and encourage students to give reasons for their answers (e.g. Why would you walk away? Why not look at the watch?).

STAGE 5: OPTIONAL EXTENSION
- Students each write one question. If you like, give students situations on a piece of paper (e.g. You need money for a telephone call).
- With a small class, let students move freely round the room asking their questions to other 'strangers'. With a larger class, they could take it in turns to choose another student and ask their question.

B Fast food survey
A man answers a market researcher's questions about fast food. He speaks with a slight London accent.

> **Key vocabulary: types of fast food**
>
> | | |
> |---|---|
> | pizza | chips |
> | burger | kebab |
> | sandwich | |
>
> *Other new words and phrases*
>
> | | |
> |---|---|
> | at lunchtime | convenient/convenience |
> | send out for | litter (bin) |
> | main meal | packaging |
> | snack | |

STAGE 1: PRE-LISTENING DISCUSSION
- Establish what foods are shown in the pictures: kebab; sandwich (baguette), slice of pizza, burger, cup of coca cola/coffee/tea, plate of chips.
- Either ask students to make their own lists of other kinds of fast food, or build up a list together on the board. If necessary, students can write the names in their own language, and then explain in English what they are like.

Unit 3

STAGE 2: LISTENING
- If you like, read through the questionnaire to check that students understand it.
- Play the tape. Students listen and complete the questionnaire with the man's answers. Pause the tape from time to time to give students time to answer.
  Answers:
  1 Yes.
  2 Burgers, sandwiches, pizza, kebabs.
  3 More than once a week (every working day, not weekends).
  4 Around midday, and sometimes in the evening.
  5 Main meal.
  6 Convenient: 3.   Tastes good: 2.
    Good for you: 1.   Expensive: 2 (or 3).
    Creates litter: 3.

STAGE 3: DISCUSSION
- Pairwork. In turn, students ask the questions in the questionnaire, and fill in answers for each other.
- As a round-up, find out what answers the majority of the class would give.

STAGE 4: OPTIONAL EXTENSION
- Pairwork. Students think of other interesting questions to ask about eating habits, and construct a questionnaire of their own. If necessary, help them by eliciting possible topics first (e.g. eating sweet things, healthy food, eating in restaurants, cooking yourself, favourite food and drinks).
- Students try out their questionnaire on other people in the class.

3 Embarrassing moments

A Sunday afternoon

A woman tells a story of how some people came to visit her by mistake. In this activity, students have to follow the 'thread' of a story and predict what will happen next.

New words and phrases	
sleepy	Good gracious!
peace and quiet	chatting
vehicle	shocked
elderly	embarrassed
cardigans	

STAGE 1: PRE-LISTENING DISCUSSION
- With books closed, tell the class an anecdote about an embarrassing experience (you could use one of the examples in the book). Use it to elicit the words 'embarrassed' (Ask: How do you think I felt?) and 'embarrassing'.
- Pairwork. Ask students to think of other embarrassing situations. They could do this in their own language, and then use English to report back to the class.

STAGE 2: LISTENING
- Play Section 1, more than once if necessary. Ask a few questions to check comprehension (e.g. What day was it? Where was the woman?). Then ask students to guess what will happen next (the unfinished sentence for Section 2 will give a clue to this).

- Play Section 2. Establish how the unfinished sentence should continue (Suddenly I heard a large vehicle arriving, and a knock on the front door.). Again ask students to guess what will happen next.
- Continue in this way through the whole story. Possible ways of completing the sentences:
  3 I opened the door, and I saw twelve elderly ladies.
  4 They said, 'Sorry we're late but we couldn't find the house.'
  5 So I asked them into the house.
  6 When my husband came back, they didn't speak to him / he looked shocked.
  7 Then we discovered that they were at the wrong house.
  8 So they were very embarrassed, and they left.

STAGE 3: LISTENING FOR DETAILS
- Look at the pictures. Ask what they show, and how they fit into the story.
  Answers:
  – the front door of the woman's house (the elderly ladies knocked at the front door)
  – hat (they were wearing hats)
  – cup and saucer (they said her husband had invited them to tea)
  – photo of the woman's children (they asked her about her children)
  – coat (they took off their coats and sat down)
  – handbag (they were carrying handbags)

- Sunday newspaper (the woman was reading Sunday newspapers in her garden)
- her husband (he arrived home later)
* Play the recording of the complete story. If necessary, pause where the items in the pictures are mentioned, and focus on what the woman says. Alternatively, let students just listen to the whole story without stopping.

B Two stories

Two anecdotes about embarrassing occasions. Students listen and make predictions.

New words and phrases	
take…for a walk	gave her a surprise
got into a fight	crept up behind her
break them up	tugged
got hold of	to my horror
knickers	false hair

STAGE 1: PRE-LISTENING: PREDICTING THE STORY
* Ask students to say what is happening in each picture, and to guess what is just about to happen.

    Possible answers:
    A There are people sitting and walking in a park; a woman and a man are both taking their dog for a walk; the dogs are looking at each other. (Maybe the dogs will fight; maybe they will make friends; maybe the owners will start talking.)
    B A woman is shopping in a supermarket; a man is standing behind her; he's stretching his hand out to touch her. (The woman will probably turn round; maybe they are friends, and the woman will say 'Hello'; maybe the man will say something to her.)

STAGE 2: LISTENING
* Before you play each story, read through the questions, so students know what to listen for.
* Play the first part of each story and answer the questions.

    Answers:
    Story A
    In a park. She was taking her dog for a walk.
    It was summer. Very hot.
    Reading, half asleep, listening to radios.
    They started fighting.
    Story B
    In a supermarket. He was shopping.
    A young woman he thought he knew.
    She was short, with long blonde hair.
    Pull her hair (as a joke).

STAGE 3: PREDICTING THE ENDINGS
* Students write an ending for each story.
* Ask a few students to read out their endings. Try to get a variety of different ideas. (Ask: Did anyone think of a different ending?)

STAGE 4: LISTENING
* Play the complete stories and ask the class to complete the sentences.

    Answers:
    A Because the woman lost her skirt and because everyone was watching.
    B Because the woman was a stranger and because the man pulled her false hair off.

4 Conversations in public

A Background noise

Three conversations in public places. This gives practice in listening to conversational English against background noise.

Key vocabulary: background noises	
The sound of	traffic
	people chatting

Other new words and phrases	
stopping train	traffic lights
main road	lose the way
you can't miss it	I doubt it

STAGE 1: PRE-LISTENING FOCUS: BACKGROUND NOISE
* Either alone or in pairs, students write down as many sounds as they can think of for the three places.
* Ask students what ideas they had. Help them with expressions they don't know, and build up three lists on the board.

STAGE 2: LISTENING: BACKGROUND NOISE
* Play the tape, and see what noises students can identify. Add any new ones to the lists on the board.
  Some of the noises on the tape are: people walking, doors closing, an announcement;

Unit 4

traffic, a car starting, car horns; people chatting, knives and forks.

STAGE 3: LISTENING
- Read through the task for Conversation A. Then play the tape.
- Go through the answers:
  1 32 minutes past the hour; it takes 1 hour 20 minutes to get to Sevenoaks.
  2 She decides to take the train.
- Look at the map for Conversation B. Check that everyone knows where the starting point is. (If possible, copy the map onto the board before the lesson.)
- Play the tape. Students follow the route on the map.
- Discuss where the Commodore Hotel should be, and mark the man's route on your map on the board.
- Read through the questions for Conversation C. Then play the tape several times until students 'catch' what is going on.
  Answers:
  1 a   2 a   3 b   4 a

STAGE 4: OPTIONAL FURTHER LISTENING
- Play the conversations without the background noise. Use this to help students who had problems with Stage 3. You could also pause the tape at this stage and focus on particular phrases (e.g. *direct*, *stopping train*).

B Opening lines

Six short conversations at a party. This gives practice in understanding and responding to 'small talk'.

Key expressions: polite openings

| Excuse me… | It's…, isn't it? |
| I was just wondering… | Can I just ask you…? |

New words and phrases

pop up to (= go to)	optician
buffet	fascinate
log fire	department

STAGE 1: PRE-LISTENING FOCUS: OPENING LINES
- Pairwork. Students think of opening lines and write them down.
- Ask students what they thought of. If you like, build up a list of remarks on the board. Possible ideas: It's hot in here, isn't it? Do you study here? That's a beautiful pullover. Do you know many people here?

STAGE 2: LISTENING: OPENING LINES
- Play each remark in turn, repeating it if necessary.
  Discuss how friendly each remark seems to be. (*Note:* There are no 'right' answers to this – it's a matter of opinion.)
- Play the remarks again. Pause after each remark, so that students can write a suitable reply (but don't discuss the replies at this point).

STAGE 3: LISTENING: COMPLETE CONVERSATIONS
- Play the complete conversations. Pause after each one and answer the questions.
  Answers:
  1 A coffee with milk and no sugar.
  2 It's got a marvellous view.
  3 (a) In London. (b) At a party in the country.
  4 Optician.
  5 No, he's just moved.
  6 A friend's.
  You could also ask further checking questions, e.g. 2 Where do you think the party is?
- Ask students what replies they wrote for each opening line.

STAGE 4: EXTENSION
- In a small class, let students move freely round the room as if they were really at a party. In a large class, ask two or three students to come to the front in turn and improvise conversations.

5 Views

A View over Athens

A Greek woman describes the view from her flat in Athens. She speaks English with a slight Greek accent.

New words and phrases	
four-storey building	smog
annoying	drastic
loudspeakers	polluted
service	breathe

STAGE 1: LISTENING FOR THE GENERAL IDEA

- As a lead-in, ask students what they know about Athens. Build up notes on the board (e.g. capital of Greece, ancient temples, polluted, built on hills, near the sea).
- Look at the pictures and ask what they show.
  Possible answers:
  a) a harbour, ships, buildings
  b) a beach, people sunbathing and windsurfing
  c) The Acropolis (an ancient Greek temple)
  d) buildings, a hill with a church on the top
  e) a church tower
  f) a street café
- Play the tape. Students listen and identify the pictures (they do not need to understand everything at this point).
- Go through the answers:
  1 e   2 a   3 c   4 d
  Not mentioned: b, f

STAGE 2: LISTENING FOR DETAILS

- Play the tape again, pausing every now and then. Ask how the pairs of words are connected.
  Expected answers:
  – her room is on the top floor of her parents' house
  – they put loudspeakers outside the church on Sunday mornings
  – the lights of the cars form colours in the streets at night
  – early in the morning there's often smog over the city
  You could also ask other questions at this stage to check detailed comprehension, e.g. How many floors does her building have? Why does she like her room? Does she like the loudspeakers? Why not?

STAGE 3: EXTENSION

- To show what to do, write brief notes on the board describing the view from your own house or flat (e.g. a busy street, cars, people shopping, a baker's shop, a tree). Using the words you have written, describe the view to the class.
- Give time for students to write similar lists of words.
- Students describe the view from their house or flat, using their notes. Either do this as pairwork or with the whole class.

B Views of Britain

Three people describe their favourite views.

Key vocabulary: features of scenery	
See words listed in Stage 1.	
Other new words and phrases	
overlooking	lashes down
low/high tide	misty
the setting sun	background
disclosed (= revealed)	range
panorama	constantly
spectacular	

STAGE 1: PRE-LISTENING FOCUS ON VOCABULARY

- Look at the list of words, and ask students to find them in the pictures. Explain any that are new (e.g. *estuary* = where a river flows into the sea; *mud flats* = flat areas of mud).
  Answers:
  a) a lake, mountains
  b) an estuary, mud flats, (the sea)
  c) the sea, cliffs, (an estuary)

STAGE 2: LISTENING: SENTENCES

- Play the sentences. Students complete the table.
- Play the tape again, and go through the answers.
  Answers:
  1 b, (a)   2 a   3 b, (c)   4 c   5 a, b, c
  6 a, b, c   7 a, b, c   8 a   9 a, b, c
  Explain any new words as you go through (e.g. *is reflected* = as in a mirror; *looks out over* = has a view of; *spectacular* = very striking, you have to notice it).

Unit 6

STAGE 3: LISTENING FOR THE GENERAL IDEA
- Play the complete descriptions. Pause after each one and ask students to identify the picture.
  Answers:
  1 b   2 c   3 a

  Note: It isn't important for students to understand every word of the descriptions at this stage.

STAGE 4: LISTENING FOR DETAILS
- See how many of the questions students can answer. Then play the tape, pausing to focus on the answers.
  Answers:
  1 Over the river; west (you can see the setting sun).
    The mud flats appear, and the sun is reflected in the mud.
  2 The view (you can see the sea, cliffs, and beaches).
    Sitting in a chair and looking out of the window.
  3 Because it changes all the time, as the weather changes.
    Sometimes raining, sometimes sunny, sometimes misty.

STAGE 5: OPTIONAL EXTENSION
- You can do this activity as a guessing game. To show students what to do, describe a view that most of the class know, but without saying where it is (e.g. There's a wide river, and an old bridge over it…). Ask the class to guess where it is.
- Students think of a view they know well, and write a few notes in preparation.
- Students describe their view to the person next to them. The other person tries to guess where it is.
- Ask a few students to describe their view to the rest of the class, who try to guess where it is.

6 On the line

A Answerphone messages

Seven messages left on a woman's answerphone. This gives practice in listening to telephone language, and in catching the main message and making notes.

Key vocabulary	
cancel	tailor
appointment	illustrations
arrange	arrangements

Other new words and phrases

do a fitting (= try on a coat)
have people round (= invite)
a walkabout (slang = a walk)

OPTIONAL LEAD-IN
Ask if any students (or their parents) have an answerphone, and why they find it useful.

STAGE 1: LISTENING FOR THE MAIN MESSAGE
- Play the tape, pausing after each section. Students listen and note down the main message. Emphasise that there is no need to understand everything at this point.
- Play the tape again. Go through the answers and write them up on the board.

Possible answers:
2 Someone she met on holiday. Wants to stay the night. Will ring again in half an hour.
3 Tailors. Call in tomorrow to try coat.
4 A friend. Meet for a drink during the week.
5 A friend. Dinner on Friday at 7.30.
6 Publisher. She's interested in illustrations. Ring her soon (name is Claire Dunne).
7 (See 2.) Meet him at Victoria Station café at 8.00 p.m.

STAGE 2: SELECTIVE LISTENING
- Ask students to imagine that today is Monday. Then play the tape again. This time students listen only for the things that Jill needs to take action on. They make notes as if in a diary.
- Go through the answers and write them on the board.

Possible answers:

Monday	Ring John Gregson (meeting)
	Arrange drink with Liz?
	Ring Steve (dinner)
	Meet Roger at 8?
Tuesday:	Go to Whites (coat)
	Ring Claire Dunne
Wednesday:	Meet John Gregson and Sue, lunchtime
Friday:	Dinner with Steve 7.30

STAGE 3: EXTENSION
- Ask students to write down everything they know (or can guess) about Jill Brown.
- When students are ready, they can turn to the person next to them and compare what they wrote.
- Ask students to tell you what they wrote. Build up a list on the board, e.g.:
  - She lives in London.
  - She's an artist.
  - She does illustrations for books.
  - She works at home. (?)
  - She's quite well off. (?)
  - She's single. (?)
  - She went on holiday to Greece recently.

B Phone calls

Students hear one side only of several phone conversations. They have to interpret what the people are talking about from the limited information they hear.

Key expressions: telephone language

We must meet up.
I'll give you a ring.
Thanks for ringing.
It's lovely to hear from you.
I'll let you know when I'm coming.

STAGE 1: LISTENING FOR THE GENERAL IDEA
- Read through the questions, so that students know what to listen for.
- Play the tape, pausing after each conversation. Students write numbers by the questions.
- Play the tape again, and go through the answers.

Answers:
1 met Anna at a party; has just moved to the same town.
2 wants to speak to Jimmy; is a complete stranger.
3 has just returned from abroad; is meeting Anna the next day.
4 has just been on a car journey.
5 is recovering from 'flu; was planning to go swimming with Anna.

Make sure students understand the sentences Anna says which give the answers:

Answers:
1 'That's right, Peter's party', 'So you'll be staying here for some time?'
2 'There's nobody called Jimmy living here.'
3 'And how was Italy?', 'See you tomorrow.'
4 'It must have been pretty awful on the motorway.'
5 'Joe said that you were still in bed.'

STAGE 2: LISTENING FOR DETAILS
At this stage, students try to get as much information as they can from what they hear.
- Play the conversations again, pausing after each one. Students make notes about the person Anna is speaking to: things they are sure about, things thay can guess, or things that are not clear.
- Discuss together what students think they know. Then play the conversations a final time to check.

Possible answers:
1 They met at Peter's party; it was some time ago; the person has come here to work (?); he/she wanted to meet on Saturday.
2 The person's got the wrong number; man or woman? Who's Jimmy?
3 The person was at a conference; gave a lecture; he/she is a close friend; they often meet for lunch.
4 The person was visiting/staying with Anna, and has arrived back home; he/she drove back through the rain; lives some distance away.
5 The person has had 'flu for several days; is still feeling quite ill; often goes swimming with Anna.

OPTIONAL EXTENSION
- In pairs, students make up a telephone conversation and write it down.
- They read out one half of the conversation only, and the rest of the class try to guess what it's about, who the person is talking to, etc.

7 Intruders

A Scare stories

Two people tell stories of times when they felt scared. Students listen to the stories in sections and predict what will happen next. In the first story, the speaker is German, and speaks with a slight German accent.

Key vocabulary	
basement	flapping
burglar	a bat
rushed out	petrified
relieved	the covers (of a bed)
dial (a number)	dragged

STAGE 1: LISTENING AND DISCUSSION
- Tell the class they will hear the beginnings of two stories.
- Play the beginning of the first story. Ask a few questions to check comprehension (e.g. Where was he? Why? Where were his parents? What did he hear?).
- Ask students what they would do. Try to get a range of ideas, and encourage students to say say why.
- Do the same with the beginning of the second story. Again, ask questions to check comprehension (e.g. What time was it? What did she see? What was it doing? How did she feel? Why?), and ask students to say what they would do.

STAGE 2: PREDICTING THE STORIES
- Look at the pictures, and ask what they show: someone in bed, hiding under the blanket (the *covers* or *bedclothes*); dialling a number; switching a light on; knocking on a door; holding a gun.
- Ask students to guess how the stories might continue, and how they might include the actions shown in the pictures (e.g. maybe the woman in bed shoots the bat).

STAGE 3: LISTENING AND PREDICTION
- Play each story section by section. After each section, ask a few questions to check comprehension, then ask students to guess what will happen next.

STAGE 4: EXTENSION: STUDENTS TELL THEIR OWN STORIES
- Divide the class into pairs. Students think of a true story, using one of the topics given. With their partner, they practise telling the story.
- Ask for volunteers to tell their story to the rest of the class.

B Jigsaw story

A woman tells a story of how a burglar broke into her flat while she was asleep. Students hear fragments of the story, and try to piece it together. The person telling the story speaks with a slight Northern English accent.

Key vocabulary: action verbs	
clattering around	wriggle
struggled	dash out
wrestled	rush after someone
Other new words and phrases	
became aware of	bulging plastic bags
suspicious	hardware
on the threshold	a quarrel

PRE-LISTENING: VOCABULARY FOCUS
- Write the key verbs (see box) on the board and make sure students understand what they mean: *clattering around* = moving and making a noise; *struggle*, *wrestle* = fight; *wriggle* = twist from side to side; *dash*, *rush* = run quickly. If possible, give examples of the verbs or translate them.

STAGE 1: LISTENING: ISOLATED SENTENCES
- Read through the questions.
- Play the tape. Emphasise that the sentences are *not* in the correct order. Pause after each sentence, and see if students can guess the answers to any of the questions. Add other questions of your own to prompt ideas, e.g.:
  Who was the man? Why do you think she felt angry?
  Who do you think opened the bedroom door? Why?
  What was in the bags, do you think? Why did he rush out? Why did she want him to stop?
- The class should gradually build up a clearer and clearer picture of what is going on. At the end, go through all the questions.
  Answers:
  This happened at the woman's flat in the morning. She was asleep. The man was stealing things from the flat. They were strangers. She wasn't pleased to see him. She was angry. She

attacked him. The man ran away. The neighbour didn't do anything.

STAGE 2: LISTENING: THE COMPLETE STORY
- Play the whole story, pausing every now and then to give students time to complete the summary.
- Look at the summary with the class and discuss what should go in the gaps.
  Possible answers:
  A woman was alone in *her flat* when she heard *someone moving in the rooms*. Then she saw *a man standing in the doorway holding two plastic bags*. So she *rushed at him and tried to fight him*, but the man *kept holding the bags*. In the end, the man *dropped the bags and dashed out of the flat*, and the woman *rushed after him screaming 'Stop!'* The neighbour had thought *it was a domestic quarrel between her flatmates*.

STAGE 4: OPTIONAL EXTENSION: ROLE-PLAY
- Ask two good students to come to the front of the class. One plays the role of the woman in the recording, the other is a police officer. The woman tells the officer what happened, and the officer asks questions.
- Divide the class into pairs. They act out a similar conversation. Alternatively, ask a few pairs to act out the conversation in front of the class.

8 Childhood

A Buried treasure

A woman tells an anecdote about her childhood. This activity gives practice in listening and following the main events in a story. The pictures are intended to give support during the listening stage, and can also be used at the beginning for vocabulary preparation.

New words and phrases	
picnic	unconscious
orange juice	bury
biscuits	leaves
pickaxe	ditch
ploughed field	groaned
gold	dug…up
knocked…out	

OPTIONAL LEAD-IN
Talk about the idea of buried treasure. Discuss with the class how children imagine buried treasure, where it is found in children's stories, etc.

STAGE 1: PRE-LISTENING DISCUSSION
- Look at the pictures and ask questions to establish what they show, e.g.:
  1 How old do you think the children are? What are they carrying?
  2 What's she giving her? Why?
- Ask students to suggest what they think happens in the story. Try to get two or three different ideas.

STAGE 2: LISTENING
- Play the tape once through. Then play it again, pausing every now and then, and get students to give you the basic facts of the story, e.g. There were three sisters. They went to find buried treasure. They came to a field. They wanted to break the stones with a sledgehammer…

STAGES 3 & 4: LISTENING FOR DETAILS
- Ask how the key words fit into the story.
  Answers:
  They took some biscuits to eat.
  They took a sledgehammer with them to help with finding treasure; the woman's sister hit her on the head with the sledgehammer.
  They found some stones at the edge of a ploughed field.
  They thought they would find gold in the stones.
  They covered her with leaves.
  She told her mother, 'I walked into a tree.'
- Play the sentences on the tape, and check that students understand exactly what the speaker says.

STAGE 5: OPTIONAL EXTENSION
- Give time for students to think of an event in their childhood and to note down key words they will need to tell the story.
- Students either form pairs to tell each other their story, or they can sit in larger groups, and tell their stories round the group.
- As a round-up, ask for volunteers to tell their story to the whole class.

Unit 9

B Party games

Four children explain how some party games are played. This part of the unit gives practice in following simple explanations. Two of the children speak with Scottish accents.

> **Key vocabulary**
>
> The objects shown in the pictures.
>
> *Other new words*
>
> | raw | messy |
> |---|---|
> | hard-boiled | wrap…up |
> | crack | neat |

STAGE 1: PRE-LISTENING DISCUSSION
- Look at the pictures and check that students understand what all the objects are.
- Ask students to try to guess how the four games might be played (you could either ask for suggestions from the whole class, or let students do this in pairs). Try to get a few different ideas for each game.

STAGES 2 & 3: LISTENING
- Play the tape, pausing after each description. Ask the class how each game is played. If necessary, help them by asking simple questions e.g.:
  What's the game called? ('Hunt the thimble')
  What happens first? (One person goes out of the room.) What do the others do? (They hide the thimble.)
- Play the tape again. Students listen and complete the table.
- Go through the answers.
  Answers:
  One person leaves the room: A
  You choose a friend to play with: D
  You have to be quick: B, D
  You have to wait your turn: B, C
  The first person to finish wins: D
  You get in a mess: C, (D?)

STAGE 4: OPTIONAL EXTENSION
- Students work in pairs. They tell each other about a party game they know, and try to explain how it is played.
- As a round-up, ask a few students to describe their games to the whole class.

9 Bought and sold

A Morning market

This activity is based on a real radio programme in England, in which people buy and sell things over the radio. It gives practice in listening for specific information and note-taking. Some of the speakers in the recording have a slight London accent.

> **Key vocabulary (for Part A and Part B): objects**
>
> | keyboard | box of chocolates |
> |---|---|
> | wardrobe | computer |
> | dressing table | tractor |
> | fridge | straw hat |
> | guitar | walkman |
> | saddle | |
>
> *Other new words and phrases*
>
> | synthesiser | drawers |
> |---|---|
> | battery | in working condition |
> | instruction booklet | leather |
> | veneer | adult |

STAGE 1: VOCABULARY FOCUS AND DISCUSSION
- Ask students to look up the English names of the objects in their dictionaries. Or simply ask the class which objects they know the names of, and present any that are not known. The objects are:
  box of chocolates; toy tractor; walkman (cassette player); dressing table; saddle; straw hat; keyboard; refrigerator (fridge); computer; table lamp; wardrobe; keyboard (synthesiser); guitar.
- Pairwork. Students go through the list of objects, saying which ones they own themselves and which are owned by someone they know. This is simply a quick way of using the vocabulary.
- Ask students to imagine they could have any one of the objects that they don't have already. Ask a few students round the class which they would choose, and why.

STAGE 2: LISTENING FOR THE GENERAL IDEA
- Explain that students will hear part of a radio

programme. Then play the tape once through, and answer the questions.

Answers:
- The purpose of the programme: people use it to buy and sell things.
- The items for sale: two keyboards, wardrobe; dressing table, fridge, guitar; saddle.

Note: At this stage there is no need for students to understand details.

STAGE 3: LISTENING FOR DETAILS
- Play the tape again, pausing where necessary and repeating sections if you need to. Students listen and write notes in the table.
- Go through the answers, playing the tape again to check. Build up a table on the board.

Answers:
Sue 1 Keyboard. Yamaha C501, mini-synthesiser, battery. £30.
     2 Keyboard. Casio NT205, with mains unit. £70.
     3 Wardrobe. Veneer, 1950s style. £12.
Nick 1 Dressing table. Modern, 4 foot long, 4 drawers. £20.
     2 Fridge. Indesit, in working condition, 10 years old. £30.
     3 Guitar. 6-string, with case. £25.
Julie Saddle. English leather, 40cm seat, adult size. £75.

STAGE 4: OPTIONAL EXTENSION
- Students write down three objects they'd like to sell.
- Students sit in groups of 5 or 6. In turn, they describe their objects, and see if other students want to buy them.

Alternative: In turn, students come out to the front and try to 'sell' their objects to the rest of the class.

B What do you think of it?

Five short conversations, about the remaining objects in the pictures. This gives practice in listening and interpreting what people are talking about.

Key vocabulary

The objects shown in the pictures (see Part A).

Other new words

to store (= keep)   cassettes
shopping list   headphones
kid (= child)   plug in
hook

STAGE 1: LISTENING FOR THE GENERAL IDEA
- Play the conversations, repeating them if necessary. Pause after each one, and ask students to say which objects the people are talking about. Ask them what the person said that told them the answer.

Answers:
1 box of chocolates ('they'll all be gone in a day')
2 computer ('typing out letters', 'storing the letters', etc.)
3 toy tractor ('for…my brother's little boy', 'push it along', etc.)
4 straw hat ('going to wear it on the beach', 'keep the sun off me')
5 walkman ('you put your cassettes in the front')

STAGE 2: LISTENING FOR DETAILS
- Read through the questions. See how many of them students can answer without hearing the tape again.
- Play each conversation again and check the answers.

Answers:
1 His girlfriend's mother. He's going to stay for the weekend. £5.99.
2 Himself. Typing and storing letters, keeping bills, shopping lists, etc. Just over £1,000.
3 Her nephew, Robbie. You can push it along and hook things onto the back.
4 Himself. Minorca (to stay with friends). He'll wear it on the beach.
5 Himself. He'll listen to music. You put the batteries in, put a cassette in, plug the headphones in, and push the button.

STAGE 3: OPTIONAL EXTENSION
You can play this game either as pairwork or with the whole class.
- Give time for students to prepare: they choose one of the objects in the pictures and think of a few things to say about it (they could write brief notes to help them).
- Choose a student to talk about his/her object, but without saying what it is. The rest of the class tries to guess what the object is.
- If you like, continue the game with other objects that students think of themselves.

10 Behind the picture

A Blackhouse

An interview with a woman who lives in a village in the Western Highlands of Scotland. She talks about an old photograph which shows her house as it was 100 years ago. Before they listen, students discuss the photo themselves. This stage is important as a way of focusing on the picture and preparing for the listening.

Key vocabulary	
tinkers	buckets
gypsies	thatched
wander about	smoky
pots	album

STAGE 1: PRE-LISTENING DISCUSSION

- Discuss the questions round the class (or let students work through them in pairs first, and then discuss them together). There are no 'right' or 'wrong' answers: the aim is just to get students thinking about the photo.
  If you like, introduce some of the vocabulary at this stage, e.g. *tinkers* = people who sell pots and buckets; *thatched roof* = a roof made of straw.

STAGE 2: LISTENING

- Play the tape and get students to listen for the answers the woman gives.
- Go through the answers. As you do this, play the tape again, pausing frequently to focus on what the woman says.
  Answers:
  1 100 years old.
  2 In Scotland. (A cold country, in Europe.) In the country (a village).
  3 They're poor. She's selling the pots and buckets – she's a tinker. (They don't live in the cottage.)
  4 It's a simple house, made of stone, with a thatched roof. Probably not very pleasant to live in – dark, smoky, shared with animals.
  5 Because they were very smoky inside.

STAGE 3: LISTENING

- Read through the incomplete sentences, so that students know what to listen for. Then play the tape once through.
- Play the tape again. Students listen and complete the sentences.

- Go through the answers, playing the tape again to check if you need to. It's important for students to catch the idea, but not to repeat the exact words the woman uses.
  Possible answers:
  A man found the photographs in *an album*. He decided to go *to the places where the photos were taken*. He visited the woman and *showed her one of the photographs*. He asked her if she knew *where it was taken*. When they went outside, they realised that *it was the woman's own house*.

B The Scream

A man talks about 'The Scream', by the Norwegian expressionist artist Edvard Munch (1863–1944). This is one of Munch's best-known works, which he did in several versions; this version is a pen and ink drawing. As in the previous activity, students look at the picture and discuss it before they listen to the tape. The man speaks with a Scottish accent.

Key vocabulary: words describing feelings	
See Stage 1 below.	
Other new words and phrases	
powerful	suffering
figure (= person)	the public (= other people)
screaming	
innocent bystanders (= people not involved in the action)	design

STAGE 1: PRE-LISTENING DISCUSSION

- Establish the meaning of the word 'scream'. Ask: When do people scream? (e.g. when they're terrified, in pain, or desperate).
- Discuss the questions round the class (or let students work through them in pairs first, and then discuss them together). Again the aim of this is to focus on the picture and prepare students for the listening phase – there are no 'right' or 'wrong' answers. Encourage students to think and express their opinion (e.g. 1 Who thinks it's a man? Could it be a woman? How can you tell?).
  When you come to Question 6, write the nouns

with their adjectives on the board. Give
examples to show their meaning:

loneliness – lonely   fear – afraid
sadness – sad   anger – angry
despair – desperate   depression – depressed
beauty – beautiful   happiness – happy

STAGE 2: LISTENING
- Play the tape and get students to listen for the answers the man gives.
- Go through the answers. As you do so, play the tape again, pausing to focus on what the man says. The man's answers:
  1. A man or a woman (he says 'figure' and 'his or her').
  2. A bridge (or perhaps a road). Sea, river or lake – he doesn't say.
  3. The person is running off the bridge.
  4. They're probably 'innocent bystanders' (they have no connection with the person). They don't know he/she is screaming.
  5. The person is hiding, so that other people won't know he/she is screaming.
  6. Loneliness, sadness, (despair, depression).

STAGES 3 & 4: LISTENING AND DISCUSSION
- Look at the picture with the class. Discuss which lines are horizontal, vertical, and diagonal.
  Answer:
  Horizontal: the sky, the sea. Vertical: the field (or wall or hill) at the side. Diagonal: the bridge or road.
- Play the tape and establish what the speaker says about the lines.
  Answer:
  They're very strong; they add to the feeling of depression; they emphasise the feelings expressed by the picture.
- Finally, ask students if they like the picture, and whether they think it's good. Encourage them to give reasons for their opinions.

11 Believe it or not

A Macbeth

A woman talks about superstitions among actors connected with Shakespeare's play 'Macbeth'. This section can also be used as a starting point for a general discussion about superstitions. The recording contains a number of unfamiliar words and phrases. Many of these are given on the page, so students can read them before they listen to the tape.

New words and phrases	
mention	mistakenly
by mistake	beheaded
dressing room	audience
clockwise	stabbed
shield	

Difficult expressions

shrug it off (= say it doesn't matter)
stick to the rules (= obey the rules)

STAGE 1: PRE-LISTENING DISCUSSION (OPTIONAL)
This is a 'brainstorming' activity, to start students thinking about superstitions.

- Write two headings on the board: 'Good luck' and 'Bad luck'. Ask students to suggest a few objects, actions, etc. to go under each heading (e.g. a black cat, number 13, throw salt over your shoulder).
- Working alone or in pairs, students think of other things that bring good or bad luck, and write them down.
- Ask students to say what they wrote, and add to the lists on the board. Ask students if they really believe in any of them.

STAGE 2: LISTENING
- Write the word 'Macbeth' on the board. Ask the class what they know about it (e.g. It's a play by Shakespeare; Macbeth was a Scottish king). Explain that they will hear someone talking about superstitions connected with Macbeth.
- Read through the questions, and explain any new words (e.g. *swear* = use bad words; *shrug*: demonstrate this; *break the spell* = stop the effect of magic).
- Play the tape, more than once if necessary.
- Get answers to the questions. Then play the tape again, pausing to focus on what the woman said.

Unit 11

Answers:
1 He's said the word 'Macbeth' (which brings bad luck).
2 'The Scottish play', 'That play' or 'Mac- oh I'm not supposed to say it'.
3 Leave the room; turn round three times; swear; knock on the door. If noone says 'Come in', leave the theatre.

STAGES 3 & 4: LISTENING
- Look at the photos. First establish what is supposed to happen in these scenes.
Answers:
Sleepwalking scene: Lady Macbeth walks across the stage in her sleep, holding a candle and talking to herself.
Fight scene: The two men fight with swords, and one kills the other.
- Ask students to suggest what could go wrong in each scene. If necessary, prompt answers by asking, e.g. What about the candle? What about the sword?
Possible answers:
She might drop the candle and burn her hand (or set fire to the theatre). One man might really kill the other, or he might trip and cut himself.
- Play the tape, and establish what actually happened.
Answers:
Sleepwalking scene: Lady Macbeth caught fire.
Fight scene: A shield flew into the audience and cut off someone's head; one of the fighters was stabbed.

Background note: Macbeth was written in 1605 by William Shakespeare (1564–1616), who is considered the greatest English dramatist. He wrote 37 plays altogether. Among his most famous plays (apart from *Macbeth*) are *Romeo and Juliet*, *Hamlet*, *Othello*, *King Lear* and *The Tempest*. A brief summary of *Macbeth*: Macbeth murders Duncan, the King of Scotland, who is a guest at his castle. As a result, he becomes king, but both he and his wife (Lady Macbeth) are tormented by guilt for what they have done. Eventually, rivals to the throne attack his castle and kill him.

B Palm reading

Two different people 'read' the palm of one of the authors of this book. Students listen and judge whether the two palm readers agree. The recordings contain a number of abstract words and concepts (e.g. character, imagination), and it is important to focus on these in the pre-listening phase.

Key vocabulary

determined	practical
character	imaginative
artistic	career

Other new words

connection	well defined
wrinkles	firmly
vaguely	

STAGE 1: PRE-LISTENING DISCUSSION
- Look at the palm print (which is of the right hand), and read the explanations beside it. If necessary, explain new vocabulary (e.g. people who paint or make things or write are *creative* – they have *creativity*).
- Pairwork. Students show each other their palm. Together, they decide if it is similar to the one shown in the book.
- Quickly ask the class what similarities or differences they found, but do not go into too much detail at this point.

STAGES 2 & 3: LISTENING AND DISCUSSION
- Read through the sentences in the table. Then play the tape, pausing at the end of each section. Students listen and mark answers in the table.
- Go through the answers, and play the tape again to check. If you like, write the table on the board or show it on an overhead projector.
Answers:

	1	2
Strong character	Yes	–
Unsure of himself	–	Yes
Wasn't sure what to do	Yes	Yes
Continue in the same job	–	Yes
Two women	Yes	–
Practical	–	Yes
Imaginative	Yes (?)	Yes
He'll retire early	–	Yes

- Establish what points the palm readers agree on.
Answer:
That he wasn't sure what to do when he was younger; that he's artistic/ imaginative.
- Discuss whether they contradict each other.
Possible answer:
One says he has a strong character, the other says he's unsure of himself. Otherwise they say different, but not contradictory things.

STAGE 4: OPTIONAL EXTENSION
- Divide the class into pairs. Students try reading

each other's palm, using the illustration to help them.
- As a round-up, ask if anyone succeeded in reading their partner's palm. Ask them what they discovered about their partner's character and life.
- Finally, ask students if they believe that it is possible to tell a person's character or their future from their palm.

12 Bread and mushrooms

A Making bread

A man describes how to make a European-style loaf of bread. This gives practice in listening to instructions and understanding technical language. The recording contains some specialised vocabulary; however, this is also given on the page and can be dealt with before the listening phase.

> **Key vocabulary**
>
> Names of ingredients, equipment and cooking processes (see the words in bubbles).

STAGE 1: PRE-LISTENING: VOCABULARY FOCUS
- To lead into the topic, ask if anyone can make bread, and what ingredients are needed (flour, water, and sometimes yeast and milk).
- Look at the pictures, and ask students to say very simply what is happening in each one. As you do this, present the key words *yeast*, *dough*, *knead* and *oven* (if possible, translate them).

Possible answers:
1 Mixing the yeast
2 Mixing the flour, water and yeast
3 Kneading the dough
4 Leaving the dough to rise
5 Putting the bread in the oven
6 Taking the bread out

- Students look at the words in the bubbles, and discuss how they might fit the pictures. Students could do this in pairs, using dictionaries. Alternatively, discuss the words with the whole class. Present new words as you go through, and establish which picture each group goes with.

Answers (in order):
Picture 3, Picture 6, Picture 1, Picture 5, Picture 4, Picture 2.

Note: It doesn't matter if students can't see how all the words fit the pictures – this will become clear during the next stage.

STAGE 2: LISTENING
- Play the tape, pausing after each section. Establish which sets of words go with each picture, and how they are used (e.g. 1 You mix the *yeast* with *sugar*, and with *milk* or water. It goes a bit *liquid*. You leave it until it becomes *bubbly*.).

STAGE 3: ORAL REPRODUCTION
- Look at each stage in turn. Ask students to try to describe the stages, using the words in the bubbles. You could do this round the class, asking each student to give just one step in the process (e.g. you take a bowl; you mix the yeast with sugar).

STAGE 4: OPTIONAL EXTENSION
- Explain that the man on the tape describes a typical British method of making bread. Ask if anyone knows how bread is made in their own country, and what differences there are.

B Edible or poisonous?

A man describes four different kinds of mushroom, and explains how you can identify them. This gives practice in listening to a technical description and making notes. The mushrooms the man describes are found throughout Europe.

> **Key vocabulary**
>
> Features of mushrooms: see picture.
> Colour adjectives: brownish (= fairly brown), pinkish, greenish, whitish.
>
> *Other new words*
>
> | edible | hallucinations |
> | poisonous | shiny |
> | recognise | sponge |
> | spots | harmless |

STAGE 1: PRE-LISTENING DISCUSSION
- Look at the mushrooms. Ask students which ones they would eat. Present the words *edible*

Unit 13

(= you can eat it), *poisonous* (= it would kill you) and *harmless* (= not dangerous).

STAGE 2: LISTENING FOR THE GENERAL IDEA
- Look at the questions, and at the picture showing the parts of a mushroom. If you like, ask students if they know what these are called in their own language.
- Play the tape. After each description, pause and ask students to identify the picture. Ask if the mushroom is edible or poisonous.
  Answers:
  Top left: cep, edible. Top right: fly agaric, poisonous. Bottom left: field mushroom, edible. Bottom right: death cap, poisonous.
  Note: Students do not need to understand every detail at this stage.

STAGE 3: LISTENING FOR SPECIFIC INFORMATION
- Play the tape again, repeating each section if necessary. Students listen and complete the captions.
- Go through the answers together, playing the tape again to check.
  Answers:
  – Field mushroom: White, slightly brownish cap. White stem with a skirt. Pinkish brown gills.
  – Fly agaric: Bright red cap with tiny white spots. White stem with a skirt.
  – Cep: Smooth, shiny brown cap. Thick stem with no skirt. Pores like a sponge.
  – Death cap: White greenish cap. Whitish green stem with a skirt. White bag at the bottom of the stem.

13 Learning to draw

A The right side of your brain

An interview with an artist, who explains the importance of the right side of the brain in learning to draw. The artist is from The Netherlands, and speaks with a slight Dutch accent.

New words and phrases	
walnut	shift (= move)
calculations	secondary school
imaginary	mathematical
abstract	geared (= directed) towards

STAGE 1: PRE-LISTENING DISCUSSION
- To introduce the topic, ask how many students in the class think they can draw well. Then read out the opinions on the page, and find out how many students agree with them.
- Ask further questions to encourage students to give their own opinion, e.g. What about you? Did you learn to draw or did you do it naturally? Did you have drawing lessons at school? Did they help you?

STAGE 2: LISTENING
- Play the tape, more than once if necessary. Establish which opinions the woman agrees with. (*Answer:* the first and last; she disagrees with the second.)

STAGE 3: LISTENING
- Explain that the brain has two halves, and that scientists believe each half is used for different skills. Then look at the questions. Ask students to guess which half of the brain is used for each of the skills in the list.
- Play the tape. Then check the answers. (If possible, write the skills on the board beforehand, or show them on an overhead projector.)
  Answers:
  speaking L   dreaming R
  calculations L   reading L
  beauty R   drawing R
  sense of time L

STAGE 4: LISTENING
- Read through the question. Then play the tape.
- Discuss the answers, playing the tape again and pausing to focus on the key points.
  Possible answers:
  – Young children: they use both sides of the brain, and draw naturally.
  – 12-year-old children: they stop using the right side of the brain, and become worried about drawing.
  – Secondary school: it encourages children to use the left side of the brain.
  – Homework and mathematics: they develop the left side more than the right side.

22

EXTENSION: QUIZ
- Read through the quiz, explaining any new words (e.g. *arts/science subjects*, *team games*, *vividly*, *gestures*, *clasp*, *estimates*, *window frame*).
- Students do the quiz, working alone or with a partner, and note down their answers.
- Go through the quiz together. Find out what answers most students gave, and who is a 'right-brain' or a 'left-brain' person.

B A drawing exercise

The same artist who was interviewed in Part A gives a drawing exercise which encourages you to use the right side of your brain. Because the picture is upside down, you see it as a set of lines and shapes – so you are not influenced by your own idea of what a face should look like. This activity gives practice in following spoken instructions.

> **Key vocabulary**
>
> See expressions on the page.

STAGE 1: PRE-LISTENING: VOCABULARY FOCUS
- Make sure that students understand the expressions in the box. You can do this by holding up a drawing: hold it *upside down*, then *turn it round*; point to *the top of the drawing*; *copy* a bit of it onto the board. Draw lines on the board, and show the *spaces* between them. Draw a piece of a *jigsaw puzzle* on the board (or translate this word).

STAGES 2 & 3: LISTENING AND DRAWING
- Make sure all students have a piece of paper and a pen or pencil.
- Play the first part of the tape, if possible without pausing (if students understand the key expressions in the box, they should be able to follow the instructions quite easily). Students listen and copy the drawing.
- When most students have finished, play the last part of the tape.

STAGE 4: DISCUSSION
- Give half a minute or so for students to show their drawing to the person next to them.
- Ask students the questions. Try to get a range of opinions from the class. If you like, add other questions, e.g. Was it easy? How good was your drawing? Was it easier to copy something upside down? Why/Why not?

14 Male and female

A Men and women

A woman talks about differences she has noticed between men and women. This activity gives practice in listening to an abstract topic, but with support given by the exercises. The woman speaks with a slight Northern English accent.

> *New words and phrases*
>
> | | |
> |---|---|
> | deal with | the universe |
> | cope with | loath to (= not like doing) |
> | concentrate on | eavesdrop |
> | domestic | truthful |
> | concrete | superficial |
> | trap (= catch) | |

STAGE 1: PRE-LISTENING DICUSSION
- Read through the statements. If necessary, explain the words *upbringing*, *roles*, and *inborn* (= you are born with them).
- Either working alone or in pairs, students decide whether they agree or disagree with each statement.
- Discuss the statements together. For each one, find out if most of the class agree, disagree or are not sure. If you can, get students to give reasons for their opinions or to give examples from their own experience. (Do this by asking questions, e.g. What do you think women can do better? Why can't men do these things? What about the men in your family?)

STAGE 2: LISTENING FOR THE GENERAL IDEA
- Read the sentences in the table, so that students know what to listen for.
- Play the tape, more than once if necessary. Students don't need to understand every word at this stage – it is enough for them to understand the main points the speaker is making.

Unit 14

- Look at the table. Ask students to make sentences that match what the woman says.
  Possible answers:
  - Women are better at doing more than one thing at a time because they're used to bringing up children.
  - Men are better at reading maps because they like to make things easy to understand.
  - Women are worse at reading maps because they don't like things to be too definite.
  - Women are better at developing relationships because they find it easier to talk about personal things.
  - Women are better at developing relationships because they learn to please other people from an early age.

STAGE 3: LISTENING FOR DETAILS
- Play the tape again, pausing from time to time. Students listen and make notes on the topics.
- Discuss what the woman says about each topic, playing the tape again to check. As you go through, ask students whether they agree.
  Possible answers:
  - men washing dishes: they have to concentrate on it; they can't do other things at the same time.
  - herself washing dishes: she can talk and maybe cook at the same time.
  - men and the universe: they want to trap the universe on a piece of paper.
  - women's conversations: they quickly start to talk about personal things.
  - men's conversations: they talk about their work and interests in a superficial way.
  - men and football: it allows them to talk without saying anything important.

B Girls and boys

Three people talk about differences in the kind of games that girls and boys play. The speakers come from three different parts of Britain: their accents are Northern English, Scottish and Northern Irish.

New words and phrases	
aggressive	lenient
violent	identify with
competition	nursery
cooperatively	peer groups
skipping	re-enacting
teddy bears	

STAGE 1: PRE-LISTENING DISCUSSION
- Look at the pictures. Establish what games the children are playing.

Answer:
Girls: fighting, Superman. Boys: skipping, playing with dolls.
- Get reactions from the class. Ask: Would you expect the pictures to be the other way round? Why? Do you think it is 'natural' for girls and boys to play different games? Ask students to talk about children they know – do the girls and boys play differently?

STAGE 2: LISTENING
- Read through the sentences and present any new words (e.g. *aggressive* = wanting to fight; *cooperate* = work together, help each other).
- Play the tape and establish the main points that the speakers make.
  Answers:
  Boys run around more, they're more aggressive, they play more with weapons, they take up more space. Girls cooperate more, they're more peaceful.
- If you like, play the tape again, pausing to focus on particular things the speakers say, e.g.:
  1 The girls play in the house corner or the book corner; the boys attack each other, play Superman or Batman.
  2 Boys play games that involve competition; they use swords or guns.
  3 Boys like playing war games, they like doing physical things; girls play games with babies and teddy bears.

STAGE 3: LISTENING
- Read the three texts. Explain that what the students hear will be different from what the texts say.
- Play the tape, pausing after each section. Ask students to correct the texts, and play the tape again to check.
  Answers:
  A The teacher at the playgroup treats the boys and girls *differently*. If a girl is playing with a train and a boy wants it, the teacher *lets the boy have it*.
  B When they are very young, girls tend to copy their mothers and boys copy their fathers. Television also has a strong influence on *boys* – they copy the *men* they see on television, who are often shown doing violent things.
  C When he was very young, my son used to play *both boys' and girls' games*. But when he went to nursery he started to play *more boys' games*. At the same time, he started watching television, and this *influenced him a lot*.
- As you go through each text, ask students if they agree with what the speaker says, and why or why not.

15 Bees

A Life in the hive

A woman talks about bees, and describes what the queen, the workers and the drones do. This gives practice in listening to someone talking about an unfamiliar topic, and in noting down information. The woman speaks with a slight Scottish accent.

New words	
function	nectar
cells	to mate with
forager	

STAGE 1: PRE-LISTENING DISCUSSION
- To introduce the topic, ask if anyone knows anything about beekeeping, or knows anyone who keeps bees. (If they do, you can use them in the activity to supply answers and information.)
- Establish that there are three kinds of bee in a hive: the queen, the workers and the drones. Then ask students to try to answer the questions, working alone or in pairs.
- Discuss the questions together, and see if the whole class agrees, but do not give the answers yet, as these will be given on the tape. The point of this stage is to prepare students for the listening phase.

STAGES 2 & 3: LISTENING
- Play the tape, pausing where necessary. Students listen and make notes for each picture.
  Note: The pictures are not in the same order as the information on the tape. To make it easier for students to match the pictures with what they hear, you could give the answer to (d) (the queen laying eggs) before you begin.
- Look at the pictures together, and discuss what they show.
  Answers:
  a) workers guarding the hive
  b) workers looking after the young bees
  c) worker collecting nectar
  d) queen laying eggs
  e) dead drones outside the hive
- Look at the statements in Exercise 1, and establish the correct answers. Play the tape again, pausing to focus on what the woman says.

Answers:
1 T
2 T
3 F (The workers turn the nectar into honey.)
4 T
5 F (Drones are male bees.)
6 F (The workers' job is to guard the hive.)
7 T

B Catching a swarm

The same woman describes how to catch a swarm of bees and move it to a new hive. This gives practice in following detailed instructions and making notes. The description includes some specialised words, but most of these are given on the page.

New words (on the tape only)	
humming	squirt
overalls	sloping up

STAGE 1: PRE-LISTENING DISCUSSION
- To introduce the activity, look at the picture of a swarm of bees. Tell the class they will hear the beekeeper explaining how to catch the swarm and move it to a new hive.
- Look at the pictures. Explain that some of the objects are used for catching bees, but not others. Look at each object in turn. Ask the class if they think it would be used or not, and if so, how (e.g. you might light the newspaper with matches, and the smoke would calm the bees down).
  Note: Do not tell students the answers yet – the point of this stage is to start them thinking and make them want to listen to the tape.

STAGE 2: LISTENING AND NOTE-TAKING
- Play the tape, pausing where necessary. Students listen and make notes.
- Go through the answers, playing the tape again and stopping to focus on each main point. If possible, have the table written on the board or show it on an overhead projector, so that you can write the answers as you go through.

Possible answers:
2 Squirt the bees with sugar and water.
3 Hold a cardboard box under the swarm.
4 Cover the box with a sheet.
5 Put some honey into the hive.
6 Put a board leading into the hive.

Unit 16

- Finally, ask students which of the objects are used.
  Answer:
  Gloves, sheet, cardboard box, hat and veil, spray, honey, wooden board.

STAGE 3: OPTIONAL EXTENSION
- Students write a paragraph based on their notes. This could be given for homework, or students could work in pairs, helping each other.

16 Emergency

A Healthline

This is based on a real telephone helpline which gives advice and information on health. It gives practice in listening to technical language and understanding specific information. The recording contains quite a lot of unfamiliar vocabulary, but much of it can be guessed from the context.

New vocabulary	
symptoms	dizzy
blockage	pillows
coronary arteries	loosen
blood clot	clothing
muscle	waist
chest	patient
warning	unconscious
discomfort	artificial respiration
bursting	recovery

STAGE 1: PRE-LISTENING DICUSSION
- To introduce the topic, write the word 'emergency' on the board. Ask students to give you examples of emergencies (e.g. you fall and break your leg, there's a fire), and what they would do (e.g. call an ambulance).
- Focus on the idea of heart attacks. Read through the questions and discuss them with the class. Alternatively, let students look at them in pairs, and then discuss them together. Do not give the answers at this stage – they are given on the tape.

STAGE 2: LISTENING
- Play the tape once.
- Play the tape again, pausing each time a question is answered. Check the answers to the questions, and establish exactly what the speaker said.
  Answers:
  1 Most heart attacks are caused by blood not reaching your heart ('a blood clot…cuts off the blood supply to part of the heart muscle').
  2 You feel pain across your chest and into your arms ('a tight pain in the chest, which may spread…down the arms to the hands').
  3 Heart attacks may be sudden or gradual ('may occur suddenly…or they may develop gradually').
  4 Heart attacks can last for up to an hour ('may last for up to an hour').

STAGE 3: DISCUSSION AND LISTENING
- Ask the class what they think you should do if someone has a heart attack. Get a few suggestions (e.g. keep the person warm; call a doctor).
- Read through the remarks, and deal with any new vocabulary (e.g. *patient* = person who is ill; *pillow* = you put your head on it when you sleep). Ask students if they think each action was right or wrong.
- Play the tape, pausing if necessary. Students listen and put a tick or cross against the remarks.
- Go through the answers, playing the tape again to check what the person said.
  Answers:
  1 Right. ('Call an ambulance. Keep the patient calm.')
  2 Wrong. ('Don't travel to the doctor yourself.')
  3 Wrong. ('Lift the patient into a half sitting position.')
  4 Wrong. ('Don't give anything to eat or drink.')
  5 Right. ('Loosen tight clothing around the neck. Keep the patient warm.')
  6 Right. ('If the patient becomes unconscious, try mouth-to-mouth artificial respiration.')
- If necessary, play the tape again. Then ask students to write five things you should do if someone has a heart attack. You could give this as a homework task.
  Possible answers:
  Call an ambulance; keep the patient warm and calm; lift the patient to a half sitting position; loosen tight clothing; stay with the patient.

Unit 17

B Street incident

A man talks about a time he saw someone shot in the street. This gives practice in listening to a story and predicting what will happen next. The incident took place on November 5th – this is Guy Fawkes' (or Bonfire) Night in Britain. On November 5th 1605, Guy Fawkes tried to blow up the Houses of Parliament in London with gunpowder. People commemorate this event every year with bonfires and fireworks.

> **New words and phrases**
>
> traffic lights
> fireworks
> collapsing
> dash off (= run away)
> bleeding
> knelt (*past of* kneel)
> mouth-to-mouth resuscitation
>
> **Proper names**
>
> South Kensington: a part of London
> Onslow Square: a square in London

STAGE 1: PRE-LISTENING DISCUSSION
- Divide the class into pairs or small groups. They read the list of incidents and decide what they would do.
- Discuss the incidents with the whole class. Try to get a range of suggestions for each (e.g. I'd shout for help, go to the nearest police station, run after them and catch them).

STAGE 2: LISTENING AND MAKING PREDICTIONS
- Play the tape, pausing after each section and discussing the questions. If necessary, play each section more than once.
  Note: Some of the questions ask students to guess what is happening or what will happen next. Possible answers are given in brackets.

Answers:
Section 1
He was in London, in his car. He was waiting at traffic lights.
He heard a bang. (Maybe it was a firework or someone shooting.)
(He got out and helped her; he looked to see who had done it.)

Section 2
He got out of his car and went to the bus stop.
She'd been shot in the head.
(The person who shot her.)
(Call the police; ask other people to help; try to stop the bleeding.)

Section 3
He ran to a hotel and asked them to call the police or an ambulance.
(They were too busy; they were afraid; they didn't care.)
(The police or ambulance will come; the person who shot her will be caught.)

Section 4
A doctor.
He gave her mouth-to-mouth resuscitation.
(The woman recovered; the person was caught and arrested; the woman gave the man £1,000 reward.)

STAGE 3: OPTIONAL EXTENSION
- Divide the class into pairs. One student in each pair is a police officer, the other is a witness. The police officer asks the witness what he/she saw.
  Alternative: Ask two good students to come to the front of the class and act out the conversation. Then repeat it with two more students.

17 Punishing children

A Smacking

The first part is a radio interview, which is based on a true newspaper report about how many parents in Britain smack their children. In the second part, four people give their opinion about punishing children. The second speaker is from Argentina, and speaks with a slight Spanish accent; the fourth speaker has a North American accent.

Unit 17

Key vocabulary	
punish	behaviour
punishment	guilty
smack	naughty

Other new words and phrases

misunderstand	drawn-out
jealous	moan (= complain)
insecure	reason with
attention	spank (= smack)
solution	

STAGE 1: LISTENING FOR THE MAIN POINTS

- To introduce the topic, write the key vocabulary on the board. Ask questions to establish what the words mean, e.g.
  - Why do parents *smack* children? When do they smack them? (To *punish* them; as a *punishment*; when they've been *naughty*, because of bad *behaviour*.)
  - The report says they feel *guilty*. Why do you think they feel guilty? (Because they think it's wrong to smack children.)
- Look at the beginning of the newspaper report. Ask students to suggest what it might say (e.g. it might say why they smack children; why they feel guilty about it; it might say why smacking is bad, or give advice to parents).
- Read through the statements, then play the tape. Students listen and mark the statements 'Yes' or 'No'.
- Go through the answers and play the tape again to check.

Answers:
1 Yes. ('nine out of ten')
2 Yes. ('only five per cent')
3 Yes. ('parents should make more effort to understand their children')
4 No. ('smacking isn't always the best solution')
5 Yes. ('it needs love and attention')

Note: The aim here is for students to catch the main points the speaker is making, so they do not need to understand every word. If you like, ask further questions to focus on other things the speaker says, e.g.: Why might a child behave badly? (Because it is jealous or insecure.) What does she say parents should do? (They should think before smacking children.)

STAGE 2: LISTENING

- Read through the four opinions.
- Play the tape, pausing after each speaker. Ask students to match what they hear with the opinions on the page.

Answers:
1 B   2 D   3 C   4 A

- If you like, play the tape again, pausing where necessary. Ask questions to focus on exactly what each speaker says: e.g. 1 What should you do? (Talk to them, explain why you're upset.) What happens if you hit them? (They learn to hit other people.)

STAGE 3: DISCUSSION

- Use the questions to find out what students think about smacking children, and which speakers they agree with. Try to get a range of opinions from the class, and encourage them to talk about their own experience. Do this by asking further questions, e.g.:
  - Do you agree? Why do you think that?
  - Why don't you agree with the last speaker? Why do you think she's wrong?
  - How did your parents punish you? Do you think they were right? Would you do the same with your children?

B Zen and the art of punishment

A woman talks about a Chinese friend who punishes his children by making them do calligraphy. The speaker is from California, and speaks with a West Coast American accent.
Note: The Chinese characters shown on the page are pronounced 'zhi ming', and mean '(having) clear ambition'. The character which the boy is writing is pronounced 'zheng', and means 'straight' or 'honest'.

New words	
traditional	stroke
calligraphy	injustice
liquid	perfection
grinding	violence
rhythmic	

STAGE 1: DISCUSSION AND LISTENING

- Look at the picture and ask what the child is doing. Establish that he's *Chinese*, he's doing *calligraphy* (= beautiful writing), drawing a Chinese *character*, using a *brush* and *ink*.
- Ask the class what they think of this as a form of punishment, and why. There is no need to go into detail about this – it is just a way of preparing for the listening phase.
- Play the tape, and ask students to complete the sentences.

Answers:
- Her friend's father was a *Chinese traditional painter*.

– As a punishment, the children had to *practise Chinese calligraphy*.

STAGE 2: LISTENING
- Read through the description. Then play the tape, and ask students to find differences in what they hear.
  Possible answers:
  1 It isn't easy.
  2 You have to make the ink yourself.
  3 You have to imagine the stroke first.
  4 You never get it exactly right.
  5 You have to do it slowly and carefully.

STAGE 3: LISTENING
- Look through the list of reasons. Then play the tape and ask students to choose the reasons the woman gives.
  Answers:
  – it makes you feel peaceful
  – it makes you forget what you did wrong
  – (it improves your mind)
  – (also, it makes you forget your anger)
- Ask students if they agree with the speaker. Ask if they know of other punishments that might have a similar effect (e.g. chopping wood, tidying your bedroom).

18 Planet Earth

A Traffic

This is a simulated radio phone-in programme on the subject of traffic congestion and pollution. It gives practice in listening to discussion and argument, and understanding people's opinions.

Key vocabulary

pollution	government
congestion	atmosphere
public transport	pedestrians

Other new words

discourage	collapse
planet	realistic
drastic	

STAGE 1: PRE-LISTENING DISCUSSION
- Write the phrases *traffic congestion* and *traffic pollution* on the board. Establish what they mean (*congestion* = too many cars on the road; *pollution* = exhaust fumes from cars making the air dirty).
- Read the seven solutions, focusing on any unfamiliar words (e.g. *limit, public transport, ban*).
- In pairs, students decide which are good solutions, and mark their answers in Column A.
- Discuss the answers together. Build up a table on the board showing the majority class opinion.

STAGE 2: LISTENING FOR THE GENERAL IDEA
- Play the tape, pausing after each speaker's opinion. Students listen and write '1' or '2' in Column B.
- Go through the answers. Only play the tape again if really necessary, as students will have a chance to hear it again in Stage 3. (At this stage, it is enough for students to get the general point each speaker is making.)
  Answers:
  Frederick Bowles (1): 4, 5, 7
  Joanna Briggs (2): 2, 3, 6
  Solution favoured by the government: 1

STAGE 3: LISTENING AND NOTE-TAKING
- Play the tape again, pausing after each of the minister's replies. Students make notes in the table or on a piece of paper.
- If you like, ask students to sit in pairs and compare what they have written.
- Discuss the answers together.
  Possible answers:
  (Spend more money on public transport): The government is already spending money on trains; most people want to use cars.
  (Make drivers pay more): Not fair to poorer people; people in the country depend on cars.
  (Discourage people from using cars in cities): The economy would collapse.

STAGE 4: OPTIONAL EXTENSION
- Look again at the solutions in Exercise 1. Ask students which of them (if any) the government is applying in their own country. Ask how

Unit 19

successful they think the government's policies are, and what else they could or should do. Tell them your own opinion, and see if they agree!

B Inside the greenhouse

Part of a radio interview, in which a man talks about the greenhouse effect and global warming.

Key vocabulary: damage to the environment

global warming	damage to crops
the greenhouse effect	drought
flooding	famine
storms	desert

Other new words

scientists
records
degrees

STAGE 1: PRE-LISTENING DISCUSSION
- Look through the list, and check that students understand the meaning of all the words (*drought* = no rain; *blizzard* = snow storm).
- Ask which are common in the students' own country, and which have become more frequent; get students to give concrete examples (e.g. two years ago, there was a drought in the east of the country).

STAGE 2: LISTENING
- Ask the class to suggest answers to the two questions. See if everyone agrees, and encourage them to say why (e.g. I saw a programme about it on TV; there was no snow last year).
- Play the tape. Establish what answers the man gives to the two questions.

Answer:
– Yes, it is getting warmer.
– Yes, there are signs of it.

- See if students can complete the sentences. Then play the tape again, and check the answers.

Answers:
– Most scientists believe the Earth is getting warmer.
– In the last 10 years, four have been the hottest since records began.
– In the next 100 years the Earth will heat up by four degrees.

STAGE 3: LISTENING
- Look at the table, and ask students to predict what the man will say. The aim of this is to focus attention on the topic and prepare for the listening phase – it doesn't matter what answers students give.
- Play the tape. Students listen and make notes in the table.
- Go through the answers, and play the tape again to check. If you like, build up a table of answers on the board or on an overhead projector.

Answers:
The sea: It will rise by 1–1.5 metres.
Coastal areas: They'll be flooded.
USA and Russia: They may suffer from drought, and stop producing food.
Mediterranean: It may become desert.
Food: Not enough will be produced – there will be famine.

STAGE 4: OPTIONAL EXTENSION
- In pairs, students read the opinions, and decide which they agree with most.
- Take each opinion in turn. Ask which pairs agree with it, and why they agree or disagree.

---

19 Sporting moments

A White water rafting

A woman describes how she went white water rafting in Costa Rica. She speaks fairly quickly with a slight Northern English accent. The activity gives practice in following the main points of a story and decoding rapid speech.

Key vocabulary: describing rivers and water

fierce	pool
cruel-looking	descent
(water)fall	foaming

Other new words	
tropical	to duck (= lower
landrover	your head)
horrific	knock yourself out
experts	helmets
untried	hillock (= small hill)
(= inexperienced)	exhilarating

STAGE 1: PRE-LISTENING DISCUSSION

- Look at the picture. Establish where the people are (on a river, in a raft, going down a waterfall), and what they are wearing (life jackets, helmets).
- Ask students whether they would find white water rafting exciting, frightening or relaxing (you can do this quite quickly, by asking students to raise their hands).
- Ask students to try to imagine what the experience of white water rafting would feel like, and then write sentences about it. If you like, guide them by suggesting ideas (e.g. What did you see/hear? Was it dangerous? What was the raft like? What was the water like? Who else was with you? What happened?). The aim of this is to give students the 'feel' of the experience, and to prepare for the listening phase.
- Ask students to read out some of their sentences.

STAGE 2: LISTENING FOR THE MAIN POINTS

- Read through the questions, dealing with any new vocabulary (e.g. *overhanging*, *branch*, *unconscious*). Play the tape through once without stopping, and see how many questions students can answer. Then play it again, pausing to focus on questions that students find hard to answer.
Answers:
1 T   2 F   3 T   4 T   5 F   6 T
7 F   8 T

STAGE 3: LISTENING FOR DETAILS

- Look at the list of adjectives and nouns. Explain any unknown words, e.g. *cruel* (give an example, e.g. being cruel to animals), *foaming* (= bubbling, like beer), *exhilarating* (= makes you excited and happy). See how many pairs students can match together.
- Play the tape again, pausing at each adjective/noun pair to check the answers.
Answers:
beautiful forests; fierce river; cruel-looking rocks; rubber rafts; quiet pool; huge (water)fall; foaming water; exhilarating feeling.

B Match of the day

Three radio sports commentaries. This gives practice in listening to fairly rapid speech and understanding important details. The first two commentaries describe real sports events that took place in 1990; the third is based on a real event, but the names of the athletes are invented.

Key vocabulary: sports expressions	
fight	World Cup
match	in first place
goal	beaten
quarter final	race
Other new words	
nicknamed	upset
advantage	cheers
alight	crowd

STAGE 1: PRE-LISTENING DISCUSSION

- Look at the pictures, and ask what sports they show.
Answers:
Sumo wrestling, football, athletics.
- Take each sport in turn, and ask students to try to tell you in English what they know about it. Help them by giving vocabulary, e.g.:
  – Sumo wrestling: two men *fight*; they try to *push* each other out of a *circle*; the one who pushes the other one out of the circle wins.
  – Football: there are two *teams*, each with eleven *players*; the players *kick* a ball, and try to *score goals*; at the end of the *match*, the team who scored most goals wins.
  – Athletics: there are usually five or six people who *race* against each other; the person who *finishes* first is the winner.

STAGES 2 & 3: LISTENING FOR THE GENERAL IDEA

- Play the tape. Students listen and match the commentaries with the pictures.
Answers:
Left – sumo; centre – football; right – athletics.
- Ask students to identify the people, and to say what country they are from. If necessary, play the tape again at this point.
Answers:
Sumo: Fujino shin (Japan), Onokuni (Japan).
Football: Roger Milla (Cameroon), Higuita (Colombia).
Athletics: Kostic (Yugoslavia), Glenda Walsh (USA), Anne Murray (Scotland).
Note: Students do not need to understand everything at this stage; it is enough for them to

Unit 20

have a general idea of what each commentary is about.

STAGE 4: LISTENING FOR DETAILS
- Play the tape again, pausing after each section. Students listen and complete the sentences.
- Go through the answers, and play the tape again to check. If possible, show the sentences on an overhead projector, and write in the complete answers as you go through.
  Answers:
  1 Onokuni, also known as *the Panda*, is fighting against Fujino shin, whose nickname is *The Truth*. Fujino shin weighs *150 kilos*, but Onokuni is *60 kilos* heavier. *Onokuni* wins the fight, because he manages to *push Fujino shin backwards*.
  2 The match is being played in *Naples*. The two teams are *Cameroon* and *Colombia*. Higuita *comes out from the goal* to try to get the ball, but this allows *Roger Milla* to *score a goal*. So the score is *two nil*, and *Cameroon* are almost certain to win. This means they will play in the *quarter final*.
  3 With 80 metres to go, Glenda Walsh is *in first place*. But *Anne Murray* overtakes her and *wins the race*. Her time is *1 minute 44.96 seconds*, which is a good win because it's only *her second serious outdoor race* this summer.

20 War zones

A Arrival in Beirut

A woman remembers what it was like to arrive at Beirut Airport in the late 1970s, during the period when there was war in Lebanon. The woman speaks with a slight New Zealand accent.

New words and phrases	
surrounded by	to greet
jeeps	constant
threatened	signposted
arrivals lounge	tense
customs officials	

STAGE 1: PRE-LISTENING: FOCUSING ACTIVITY
- Ask students to imagine the scene as they arrive by plane in their own country. You could give time for students to write down things they imagine, or you could simply get suggestions from the class and build up three lists on the board. Try to get students to 'see' the scene in detail (e.g. the runway; grass; flowers; it's raining; other planes; people on the airport building, waving; security police).
  Note: It does not matter if students have never travelled by plane – the aim of this stage is to help students imagine what an airport is like in most countries, as a contrast to what they will hear on the tape.

STAGE 2: LISTENING FOR THE MAIN POINTS
- Play the tape. Students listen and make brief notes, but at this stage they should not try to note down too much detail.
- Go through the answers together. If necessary, play the tape again to check.
  Answers:
  a) a sign saying 'Welcome to Beirut'
  b) jeeps; people in uniforms with guns, smiling
  c) crowds of people

STAGE 3: LISTENING FOR DETAILS
- Play the tape again. As they listen, ask students to notice how the speaker uses the words in the diagram.
- Discuss how the words are connected. Play the tape again. Pause each time the speaker uses one of the words, and focus on what she says.
  Possible answers:
  – People went past the customs officers.
  – People came to greet their relatives.
  – People asked you if you wanted a taxi.
  – People asked you if you wanted to change money.
  – People offered to carry your bags.
  – There was a constant noise of people.
  – She was glad to accept help from people.
  – People were very friendly.

B Northern Ireland

A woman from Belfast talks about life in Northern Ireland and how people cope with the fighting. This is more difficult than most of the pieces of listening in this book; for this reason, the exercises are designed to help students as much as